<u>This Book Is Dedicated To:</u>

"You don't choose your family. They are God's gift to you, as you are to them." – Desmond Tutu

Listen up...Here we go...

Part One:
Charged Chaos

Parents: Wow I cannot wait for Issac to open up presents to see the look on his face. Its time! Here we go., first present is up.... Issac is tearing into the wrapping and out comes what appears to be an... army men set.

Parents: "Thinking to themselves" Checking each box of the internal checklist. Does it make noise? How small are they? Choking hazard? How does his brother look? Does he think that's his gift? Hmm, pretty cool. "Mental" Thank you to the gift giver.

Issac's eyes grow and just as he sees this amazing army men set. There it goes, over the shoulder to the "okay on to the next one pile" without a thank you heard for miles.

Parents: Issac, Say thank you.

After a few rounds of this tossing contest, the last and most suspicious wrapped gift is next. Issac grabs the gift with zero hesitation and rips into the corner...

As Issac burst into excitement Mom and I experienced a cringing reaction to what looked and sounded like a screeching chicken with wings. After further examination, it was a giant T-Rex with buttons… Suspicion confirmed.

Well, Issac after the batteries die in those toys they cannot be replaced. But you can still play with it.

If you know you know.

RRA!

Part Two:
The Great Repeat

Parents: It's finally the weekend. It is time to unwind from the week-long thing we call work! It is going to be such a relaxing weekend. We get to spend all of our time here at home and catch up on time with the kids from the week...Something smells like feet.

Let us see what a typical day at home with the little ones looks like.

Parent Side Note: (read at your own risk) I can predict right now that the majority of what you are about to read has already been said in the last hour. Prove me wrong...

No
Stop
Leave your brother alone
Leave your sister alone
Clean your room
Let's go
I asked you to...
Their name x10
Get that out of your mouth
Sit up in your chair
Get over here
You can't say that
That's a bad word
Lift the seat
Wash your hands
Did you flush?
You have to eat
Finish your plate
No dessert
What happened?
Why did you do that?
Where did you put it?
Walk
Stop running
Inside voice
Really?
1,2....Who gets to 3?
Turn the light off
Close the door
Stop drinking so much you'll get full

Kids, Let's think about all these requests.

Do you *like* being asked over and over again?

Do you want more time to do the things you want to do?

Well, it's a great time to start listening, start stopping, get in that tub or shower, flush the toilet, clean your hands, understand what no means, and most importantly eat your meal when mom and dad take the time and pour their love into a meal for you.

One phrase to add to the kid's list. "I appreciate you". Appreciate your parents.

(Appreciate defined: (Is a feeling of thankfulness)

If you know, you know.

Part Three:

The Best Games

If you know,

you know.

Quick! First to pick up the toys the fastest wins!

If you know,

you know.

First one to finish their food gets *ice cream!*

If you know,

you know.

Part Four:

Shoe Toys

Whoa!

How? and why are there toys in my shoe?

Parents: let's be honest... We love the reminders of our little ones.

if you know, you know.

Part Five:

The Great Land of: The Back Seat.

Parents: Ahh. we sure do love making sure the back seats are squeaky clean. That way our kids can have a clean slate with their imaginations. A clean canvas more so.

oh...Look what I found.

If you know, you know.

Part Six:

Clean Hands, No problem.

Kids:

Who needs a napkin or a washcloth when you have a shirt and pants! It's the quickest way to clean hands.

They always end up clean by the next time I wear them.

Parents: Let's pause here and let our kids in on the "magic" of how the clothes end up clean.

If you know, you know.

Part Seven:

Kids On Demand

I am going to say it.... "Back in our day" We didn't get to choose what we wanted to watch or really have the ability to search and watch endless videos. We had to wait a whole week between our favorite shows to see the next episode.

Parents: Kids now is a good time for us to explain how mom and dad were raised. We looked at our parents as role models and wanted nothing more than to follow in their footsteps. Moderation is when we say screen time is up and you need to start a break, patience is listening and following our request without asking us if you can have more time or if time is up yet. Appreciation is thinking about and looking at all the things you have. Think about life as you currently know it. Imagine if everything was gone. When it is not screen time Use your imagination; it is that creativity you find in yourself that will lead you to your greatest ideas and accomplishments in life.

If you know, you know.

Part Eight:

The Not So Routine, Routine.

Do I have to....

Why do I always have to.....

I don't want to... (Key the tantrum)

Fine!

Not again!

If you know, you know.

Kids let's make routine things, routine. We don't want you to stink! Do you want other kids to think you stink?

We don't want you to get a toothache. Do you really want to go to the dentist again?

Trust us, we love you. We want the best for you!

So... Kids what are we going to do? Make routine things...?

Part Nine:

The Nothing

What did you do today at school?

What are you learning in math?

What did you have for lunch?

Anything you want to tell us about your day?

ummm......
Nothing
If you know, you know.

THE END